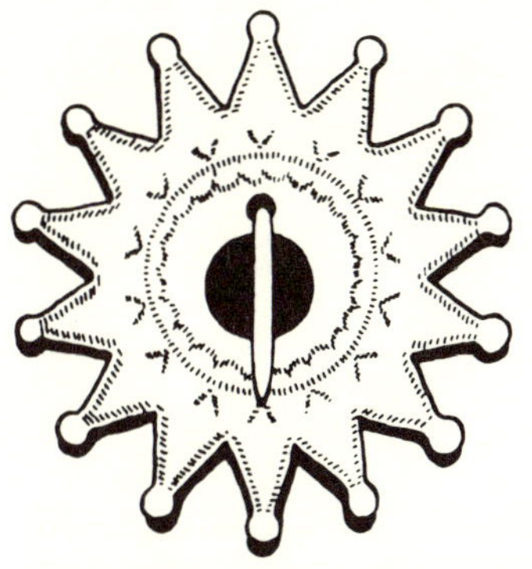

PAULINE JOHNSON

By Lucie Hartley

DILLON PRESS, INC.
MINNEAPOLIS, MINNESOTA

Dillon Press, Inc., 500 South Third Street
Minneapolis, Minnesota 55415

Printed in the United States of America

Library of Congress Cataloging in Publication Data

Hartley, Lucie
  Pauline Johnson.

  SUMMARY: A biography of the nineteenth-century Canadian poet who gained fame through her one-woman shows which brought directly to the people her verses of her Mohawk heritage and of her country.
  [1. Johnson, Emily Pauline, 1861-1913. 2. Poets, Canadian. 3. Mohawk Indians—Biography. 4. Indians of North America—Canada—Biography] 1. Johnson, Emily Pauline, 1861-1913—Biography—Juvenile literature. 2. Poets, Canadian—19th century—Biography—Juvenile literature. 3. Mohawk Indians—Biography—Juvenile literature. I. Title.
  PR9199.2.J64Z7   811'.4 [B] [92]   78-8040
  ISBN 0-87518-156-2

ON THE FRONT COVER:
Pauline Johnson in the Mohawk dress she wore for poetry recitations.

ON THE BACK COVER:
A wampum belt that represents the League of the Iroquois. Its design means "one heart for all the nations."

PAULINE JOHNSON

"The Song My Paddle Sings" by Pauline Johnson is a
poem well known to Canadians. Its author, however, was
known in her lifetime more as an entertainer than a
poet.
The daughter of a Mohawk sachem, she traveled back
and forth across Canada for more than seventeen years,
bringing her poetry to large cities and new settlements
alike. Her lilting, dramatic verses having to do with
her Native American heritage and the vast nation of her
birth, struck a deep chord in those who flocked to
see her.
Following her death in 1913, she passed into her
country's history where, for a time, she had been the
voice of Canada.

contents

CHAPTER I

Story of a Nation

The little girl and the old man spent much time together after his wife died. Sitting in the warmth of the summer sun, the old one would speak so beautifully that his stories sounded like songs. And when he finished one story, the little girl would beg for another.

The old man was Smoke Johnson, a respected Mohawk sachem, or chief. He was telling his granddaughter, Pauline, the timeless legends of his people.

Years later, this is how Pauline began a legend of her own:

> There's a spirit on the river, there's a ghost upon
> the shore,
> They are chanting, they are singing through the
> starlight evermore,
> As they steal amid the silence,
> And the shadows of the shore.

When she wrote these opening lines to her poem, "Dawen-dine," Pauline was a famous Canadian poet and a fiery spokeswoman for Native Americans. Her poems and legends were eagerly read by young people, and in her special way

Pauline, at the age for story telling.

she did for them what her grandfather had done for her.

Pauline's Indian heritage, handed down to her through her grandfather and father, was rich in history. The Mohawk tribe to which they belonged was one of the League of Six Nations of the Iroquois. The league had been formed about fifty years before Columbus stepped on American shores.

According to an old, old legend, the League of the Iroquois had its beginning in a vision that appeared to a man named Dekanawida. He saw a great spruce tree with its branches reaching up to the Master of All Life. An eagle perched at the top of the tree. Dekanawida knew that the eagle stood for peace and that the branches meant the sisterhood of all tribes. He believed he had been chosen to tell all the tribes about his dream and to urge them to join together in peace.

For hundreds of years the tribes living in the large area that is now the Labrador peninsula in Canada and the northeastern part of the United States had been at war with one another. Fighting was a means of gaining honor. For every killing there had to be a killing in return, and there was no end to it. Some wanted to stop the bloodshed, but until Dekanawida's vision, there had seemed no way to do it without dishonor.

Dekanawida went first to a Mohawk village. The war between the Mohawks and the Onondagas had gone on for so long that the people were in great need. He asked a man living in this village to make peace with his bitter enemy, an Onondaga warrior named Odarho. This man, who became known as Hiawatha, had faith in the power of Dekanawida's vision. Hiawatha and Odarho were able to unite the Mohawks and the Onondagas. Then, the Oneidas, the Senecas, and the Cayugas joined the peace, and the five tribes united into a league, which was called the Five Nations of the Iroquois.

The league was governed by a Great Council, made up of fifty chiefs, called sachems. When important decisions were made, the sachems from each tribe had one vote. The sachems were usually men, but they were chosen by the women. When a sachem died or left office, the head woman of his clan chose the one who would take his place. Before making her final decision, she discussed her choice with the other women. After a time of mourning for a dead sachem, a ceremony was held to install the new sachem. During this ceremony, the sachem was given a set of deer antlers as his badge of office. The sachem wore these antlers during council meetings. If a sachem acted unwisely the women put him out of office by "taking away the deer horns."

Ths Great Council of the Iroquois met once a year in a large meetinghouse built especially for it near what is now the city of Syracuse, New York. This was in Onondaga territory, and the Onondagas were the keepers of the central council fire. Since the sachems spoke in the Great Council as the voices of their people, they were powerful speakers.

All important records of the league, such as treaties and agreements made by the council, were kept in code by colored beads called wampum. These were made out of the thick clamshells called quahogs, in their natural colors of white, purple, and black. Women strung the beads and wove them into belts, using the colors to make patterns. These patterns took the place of writing, and it took specially trained people to "read" the meaning of the beads.

The tribes belonging to the league lived in peace with one another for many years. They thought of their League of Five Nations as the beginning of a league that would one day embrace all the world they knew. But it failed to spread, because once the five tribes had organized, they thought they should be the leaders of the league. Tribes that wanted to join later could not join as equals. The only tribe that was accepted was the Tuscarora, which belonged to the same language group. Even they had to wait for several years before they were accepted as equals and the Five Nations became the Six Nations.

After about a hundred and fifty years, white people came to the land of the Iroquois. Their first meeting was in battle. Some French explorers had allied themselves with the Algonquin tribes, the traditional enemy of the Iroquois. A battle took place in which two Mohawk sachems were killed and the Mohawks badly defeated. From this time on, the Six Nations had a deep distrust of the French.

The Dutch and the English traders were more successful in their dealings with the Iroquois. Contact with the white people changed the ways of the Iroquois. Where before they had lived in longhouses made of elm bark, now they built log cabins with fireplaces. They planted fruit trees by their fields of corn, beans, and squash. They traded furs for kettles, steel knives, cloth, and guns. Little by little, as the white newcomers cleared more and more of the forests, the game became scarce. The Iroquois had to depend more and more upon the white people.

In 1738 an Englishman named William Johnson settled in the beautiful Mohawk Valley in central New York. He

*The Iroquois people lived in longhouses, well-built homes
that had apartments for several families.*

studied Mohawk customs and learned to speak the Mohawk
language. In 1755 the British government appointed him to
be the superintendent of Indian affairs for the League of
Six Nations. This meant that all the dealings of the government with the Iroquois were carried on through Johnson.
By this time he was the owner of thousands of acres of pas-
tures, orchards, and croplands. Later, he built a stately
home, known as Johnson Hall.

Some time after the death of his wife, Johnson
married Molly Brant, a young Mohawk woman. Molly
was very popular with her people, and now she was
the mistress of a large house with a staff of many servants.
Everyone was welcome in Johnson Hall. Visitors from
England and the American colonies were entertained as
grandly as they were in the great homes of London, Boston,

and Philadelphia. Mohawks who had business with the Indian agent were shown every courtesy. And Molly told her younger brother, Joseph, that the door of Johnson Hall was always open to him. He could stay there whenever and as long as he liked. There was plenty of room and no shortage of space around the dining table. Joseph had a sharp eye and a quick mind. Molly's husband soon took an interest in the young boy's education and welfare.

Shortly after Molly's and William's marriage, war broke out between the French and the British. The French and Indian War, as it became known, raged for nine long years. At its end, the French gave up their claim to all their lands in Canada to Britain. In large part due to William Johnson, the Iroquois helped the English. He was knighted for his war service and became Sir William Johnson, Baronet.

When the threat of war once more hung over the valley, Sir William had been dead for two years, and Joseph Brant, now in his early thirties, was a Mohawk sachem and a person of great influence. After the signing of the Declaration of Independence in 1776, the fifty sachems of the Six Nations met in council and tried to decide which side to take in the war. Should they help the English, with whom they had so long been friendly, or take the side of the American colonists, who seemed, at least to some, to be right? Joseph Brant stood firmly on the side of the English. After long hours of debate, the Mohawk, Seneca, Cayuga, and Onondaga tribes sided with the English. The Oneida and the Tuscarora held out for the Americans.

It had always been a rule that in important decision making all the nations had to agree before any action was taken. Without complete agreement of all six, there was no unity, and without unity, there could be no league. After many days there was still no agreement. Sadly, the sachems put out the council fire. The confederacy was at an end.

It was a tragic time for the Iroquois. When the War of Independence was over, the village that held the meeting-house for the Great Council was in ashes. Many of the Iroquois people were hungry and homeless.

Through the efforts of Joseph Brant, the British offered the Six Nations a refuge in Canada. Some of them, with Brant as their leader, set out for a large tract of land along the Bay of Quinte and the Grand River, north of Niagara in Ontario. Fearing American soldiers, they fled secretly. They were able to take only a few belongings with them.

Catherine Martin took charge of the silver communion service, which had been a gift to the Mohawks from Queen Anne of England. Catherine hid the precious silver in a ragged bundle of clothing and carried her heavy burden on her back all the long miles to Canada. Several times the band of Indians was stopped by soldiers. Once a soldier prodded Catherine to hurry on her way by thrusting his bayonet into her bundle. The silver was scratched but not discovered, and Catherine brought it safely to the Grand River Reservation.

This courageous Catherine Martin was Pauline Johnson's great-grandmother. The last name of Johnson came into the family through Sir William Johnson, who had acted as godfather to Pauline's great-grandfather. It was due to Catherine Martin, Joseph Brant, and all the other brave people who made the dangerous journey to Canada that the Great Council met once more in a new country. Dekanawida's vision was again a reality.

CHAPTER II

Chiefswood

Emily Howells listened with excitement to the steady beat of Indian drums. She was watching the people of the Grand River Reservation gather for the ceremony of installing a new Mohawk sachem. The tall, handsome young man who had been chosen stood waiting for the ceremony to begin. He was dressed in the full costume of his rank—a fringed buckskin tunic and leggings embroidered with dyed porcupine quills and decorated with stitching of colored moose hair. In his shiny black hair was an eagle plume. On his feet were beaded moccasins. The one who would soon be a sachem was a close friend of Emily's —George Martin Johnson.

As Emily watched, the drums stopped. An old chief, a member of the Bear Clan, stepped forward and took George's hand as he began a strange, wild chant. He led George in a ceremonial walk back and forth. Then a chief of the Wolf Clan, George's own clan, and a chief of the Turtle Clan, joined the chant, and each sang a part of the ancient ritual. For a long time there was no sound except the three old voices. When the chant ended, one of the sachems placed a scarf over George's right shoulder and tied it under his left arm. The ritual was over, and George was now a sachem, a member of the Great Council.

According to custom, George had not inherited his rank. He had been named to fill an opening on the Great Council by his mother, the head matron of the Wolf Clan. It was Helen Martin's right to choose a new chief whenever a sachem from the Wolf Clan died or left office. In the years to come, Helen would disapprove of his ties to young Emily Howells. Emily had come from Ohio to live with her sister, Eliza, and her husband. Eliza's husband, Adam Elliott, was a missionary at the Grand River Reservation.

When the time came for George to marry, his parents arranged a match for him, as was the custom. They chose a young woman who was suitable in every way to be the wife of a chief. Suitable, that is, in every way but one. When George was told of their choice, he realized for the first time how deeply he loved Emily Howells. His parents were shocked when he told them he would not marry the Mohawk woman because he wanted to marry Emily. It would never do, they insisted. If a woman who was not Mohawk became the mother of his children, they, in turn, could not be considered Mohawks. George's sons would never sit in the Great Council. None of George's daughters would ever become head matron of the Wolf Clan.

Adam and Eliza were pleased at the news because they loved both of them, but at the same time, they were worried. George's parents already objected strongly. Other people, too, might not look kindly on a marriage between an Indian man and a white woman. The young couple, however, had made up their minds. George bought two hundred acres of land not far from where the Elliotts lived and began plans for the house he would build there for his bride. In spite of the disapproval of both George's family and Emily's relatives in Ohio, they were married on August 27, 1853.

Pauline was born in Chiefswood, the beautiful home that George had built for Emily, in 1861. She joined a family of two brothers, Beverly and Allen, and a sister, Evelyn.

Allen, especially, enjoyed the companionship of his younger sister. Pauline was always seeing the funny side of things and knew just how to make him giggle. One evening when the two of them had misbehaved, they were sent upstairs as punishment. So that they might think about their wrongdoing, they were told to spend some quiet time in the dark without the usual light on. The children ran outside first and collected two jars of fireflies, which they smuggled upstairs with great glee. So much for quiet thought!

But Pauline had a love of poetry that Allen couldn't understand. "Poems—always poems," he would mutter under his breath when he came upon Pauline in the schoolroom, busily scribbling with a stubby pencil on a tablet of paper. To his way of thinking, a hike in the woods was a lot more fun.

Perhaps it was her grandfather's stories that made Pauline aware of the beauty of words from her early years because when she was still quite small, she began to think up verses. She saw beauty, too, in many things around her, like the rapids on the Grand River, morning dew sparkling on a cobweb in the grass, and reeds at the edge of the river swaying in the breeze.

As soon as she could write, she wrote her poems down. She was influenced both by the Mohawk chants she learned from her grandfather and by the English poetry she had

When she grew up, Pauline looked much like her mother,
Emily Howells Johnson, as this photo of Emily shows.

begun to read. The library at Chiefswood had many books, and her mother encouraged Pauline by reading to her and having her memorize the best of the poems. So Pauline began her habit of expressing her thoughts in poetry.

Her father was an important leader of his people and a spokesman for them in dealings with the Canadian government. Chiefswood, with its spacious rooms and lovely gardens, drew a constant stream of visitors. Well-known artists, writers, and scholars came to Pauline's home. Every important person from England who visited Canada was eager to visit the beautiful Chiefswood estate. From these people Pauline learned about the world outside of Canada. Although she didn't realize it at the time, she was also becoming acquainted with people who would later be of help to her in her career.

One of those who came to Chiefswood when Pauline was a little girl was Prince Arthur, Duke of Connaught, who later became governor-general of Canada. On October 1, 1869, Arthur was made a chief of the Six Nations, the only white man ever to be so honored. Pauline's father was one of a small group of Indians from the reservation who met Arthur's train in Brantford and escorted his carriage back to the Mohawk church. There, three hundred Mohawk warriors in traditional tribal dress were waiting. The prince entered the church, where he inspected the Bible and Queen Anne's communion service. Then Chief George Johnson spread his scarlet blanket, the same one that usually draped the Johnson piano, on the ground outside and asked Arthur to stand on it. To the beat of drums the young prince was given an Indian name and made a chief of the Six Nations. The story of how a prince became a chief is one of the tales in *Legends of Vancouver,* which Pauline wrote toward the end of her life.

George Johnson's official duties took him away from home a great deal. Pauline remembered her father mainly for the walks they took together through the reservation when he taught her about the plants and animals they found. Once, they rescued a baby chipmunk whose mother had been killed. Pauline kept it as a pet. Pert and lively as its owner, the little animal had a way of getting into mischief. One day when Pauline's best friend came to visit, Pauline brought her upstairs to show her a nightgown she had made. Pauline had spent many hours embroidering it. All the way up the stairs, she told Jean how pretty it was. But when she took the gown from the drawer and shook out the folds, it fell into shreds! The chipmunk had found her nightgown to be fine nesting material. Jean burst into laughter, but this time Pauline could not join in the fun.

As a teenager, Pauline was very popular. She was always thinking of things to do, and her friends were carried along by her energy, her persuasive voice, and her merry laughter. Pauline met Jean Morton, her best friend, while she was living in Brantford and going to high school. She had gone to school for only five of her eighteen years. When she was little, she and Allen had been taught by a governess at home, and before going to high school, she had spent three years at the small school on the reservation.

Her education, however, was just beginning. In a way, she could be called self-educated, because she read so much and so widely. Poetry was always a favorite with her, and she especially admired Scott, Byron, Shakespeare, and Longfellow. Evelyn later said that often she had seen her

Pauline's father, George Johnson, in the dress of a Mohawk sachem. He is wearing the red blanket upon which Prince Arthur stood when he, too, was made a sachem.

sister lying on her bed, concentrating so hard on a book of poetry that she did not hear anyone speak. Often she would take a book with her in her canoe, paddle upstream, and then read while she drifted lazily back.

Several times Pauline joined friends on camping trips into the beautiful lake country of Ontario. The Canadian wilderness between Georgian Bay, the north arm of Lake Huron, and the Muskoka Lakes had great natural beauty, and it became the subject of some of Pauline's poems. She wrote of Muskoka as "A stream of tender gladness / Of filmy sun, and opal tinted skies; / Of warm midsummer air that lightly lies / In mystic rings."

Pauline's carefree way of life came sadly to an end one winter night. Her father had been in poor health for years as the result of vicious beatings. When George was a young man, some white people had begun to cut timber unlawfully on the reservation. George made every effort to keep these men away. He also opposed other men who sold liquor to the Indians and then tried to cheat them. In 1865, some of his enemies attacked him while he was walking home alone through the woods. The men hit him with clubs and stones, bruising him badly and breaking both his jaws. Eight years later, he was attacked again and injured so badly that he was never really free from pain. On February 19, 1884, he died of a fever that destroyed his already weakened health. He was sixty-seven years old.

The Indian death cry went up and down the Grand River from one listening point to another. A few days later Chief Johnson was buried alongside his ancestors in the little churchyard by the Mohawk Church.

CHAPTER III

A New Career

The death of Pauline's father marked a turning point in her life. Since there was not enough money to maintain Chiefswood as it had been in the past, it was rented to tenant farmers, and Pauline, Evelyn, and Emily found a small apartment in Brantford. At twenty-three, Pauline came face to face with the need to earn her own living. Her brothers had already found jobs, but Pauline's first thought was to earn money by selling her poems. Her sister Evelyn urged her to do something more practical instead, like finding an office job, as Evelyn herself had done, but Pauline had made up her mind. Jean's husband Douglas suggested some magazines she might send her poems to, and she was on her way.

It was only fitting that the first poem to be accepted for publication was one written for her best friend, Jean, years before, called "My Little Jean." Soon she was selling a fairly steady stream of poems. Although the amount of money she received for them was very small, she was making a reputation as a poet. Her talent was recognized by Pauline's own people, the Mohawks, when she was asked to write poems for two important events. One was a ceremony for the reburial of nine Seneca chiefs, whose burial grounds had been disturbed when a building project took over the land. The Iroquois tribes wanted to honor these chiefs with a peaceful resting place. Among the nine chiefs was Red Jacket, the most famous of the Seneca orators, or public speakers. Pauline's poem for the occasion was called "The Re-interment of Red Jacket." The other ceremony was the unveiling of a statue of Joseph Brant in Victoria Square in Brantford.

Then something else happened to give a push to Pauline's career as a poet. William Lighthall of Montreal put together a book of poems by Canadians, and in it he included two poems by Pauline. This was an important honor for her. In later years she called Dr. Lighthall her "literary father" and gave him credit for her real start as a poet. A copy of Light-

Pauline in 1890, when she was living in Brantford with her mother and sister.

hall's book, called *Songs of the Great Dominion,* was sent to an important literary critic in England named Theodore Watts-Dunton. He wrote a review of the book for a literary magazine, the *Athenaeum,* and in his review he gave his greatest praise to Pauline's two poems. He felt her poetry stood out from the others as sounding a fresh, new note— "the note of the [Indian's] Canada." Thus Pauline became known in England as well as in Canada.

Although Pauline was beginning to make a reputation for herself, she was still far from earning much in this way. "The Song My Paddle Sings," one of Pauline's most famous poems, brought her the sum of three dollars when it was first published. She still had to depend on Evelyn and her brothers for financial support.

Pauline in her canoe.

Then in January of 1892, Pauline received an invitation that introduced her to a new way of life. She was asked to join with a number of other poets in a verse-reading entertainment for the Young Liberal Club of Toronto. Several distinguished Canadian poets were each to read from their own poetry. Imagine how people gathered to enjoy a quiet evening of beautiful poetry must have felt when Pauline, introduced as the "Indian Poet Princess," spoke out in a strong voice—

> . . . . They all [British soldiers] are young and beautiful
>   and good;
> Curse to the war that drinks their harmless blood.
> Curse to the fate that brought them from the East
> To be our chiefs—to make our nation least
> That breathes the air of this vast continent. . . .
> They never think how they would feel today,
> If some great nation came from far away,
> Wresting their country from their hapless braves,
> Giving what they gave us—but wars and graves. . . .

In the next day's newspaper, the program was described as a little slow until Pauline took the stage. Her poems were dramatic and different, and the way she presented them was so vivid, so real, that she took her audience by storm. Pauline's new career had its beginning that night. She was to hold people spellbound, time and time again, whenever she appeared on the stage reciting her poetry. In the years to come she would become known to the Canadian people as a great entertainer.

Immediately following her success on that first occasion,

Frank Yeigh, a Toronto journalist, arranged for her to give an entire evening's performance by herself. For this event she wrote the poem for which she later became known to every Canadian schoolchild, "The Song My Paddle Sings."

> West wind blow from your prairie nest [!]
> Blow from the mountains, blow from the west.
> The sail is idle, the sailor too;
> O! wind of the west, we wait for you. . .

Pauline's first program was so successful that Frank Yeigh arranged a series of 125 recitals. During the next few months she appeared in 50 towns in Ontario and Quebec. Some people said she had inherited the talent of her grandfather, who had been known as the "Mohawk warbler." At any rate, audiences loved her, and she enjoyed using her new-found talent. Soon she became one of the most popular entertainers in Canada.

We must remember that Pauline lived in the days of the platform entertainer. There was no television or radio, and people depended upon these traveling entertainers. They visited small towns as well as great cities, giving dramatic readings, musical shows, and lectures. Their performances were called "concerts" or "shows." Such shows were given in any available place—a church hall, a schoolhouse, or even a corner set off for the purpose in a saloon. Larger towns had a building called an opera house, which had a stage, some scenery backdrops, and a canvas roll-up curtain decorated with a picture and local advertisements. Seats were usually backless planks.

For her first entertainments Pauline wore a simple white

dress. Then she decided that her Indian poems would be much more effective if she wore an Indian costume. So she set to work to design and make one herself. Her first effort, a buckskin dress with long fringes running the length of the sleeves, did not satisfy her. Then she tried making another sleeve out of cloth instead of buckskin. Finally she showed Evelyn the costume with one sleeve each way and asked her which sleeve looked better.

Evelyn studied the costume carefully, asking Pauline to turn around slowly. She liked the costume just as it was, with two different sleeves. Pauline was taken with the idea and trimmed the cloth sleeve with back-tipped ermine tails. Then she sewed silver brooches over the bodice of the dress. These were family heirlooms that had been hammered from silver coins by Indian silversmiths. Her belt and bracelets were of wampum, the white and purple shell beads that the Iroquois had used since ancient times. As a final touch, she flung over her shoulder the scarlet blanket that had draped the piano at Chiefswood. It was a dramatic, beautiful costume, and Pauline wore it for many years.

Stuck in her belt was her father's knife, which she pulled out when she recited "Ojistoh." "Ojistoh" is a ballad, or story-poem, about a woman who stabs an enemy warrior with his own knife. One winter evening after a performance that included "Ojistoh," Pauline hired a horse and carriage to take her to the railroad station. As Pauline left the opera house, muffled in her warm winter clothes, she overheard two drivers discussing the program. "Are you going to take

Pauline wearing the costume she made. The red blanket from home is draped over her shoulder.

that Indian woman to the station?" one of them asked the other. "I'm glad I don't have to. She is really fierce. I wouldn't want her sitting behind *me* with that knife!" Pauline giggled as she listened to him, but she did not tell him who she was. She was glad to hear that her performance had been so convincing!

Pauline's career as an entertainer was to be hers for the next seventeen years. Without a home of her own, she would live in trains and hotels. She would be a nomad, traveling to all parts of the country—nineteen trips across the vast stretches of Canada from coast to coast, six of them including parts of the United States. Walter McRaye, who traveled with her as her manager and a fellow performer for nine of those years, wrote later,

> Those years were packed with experiences and incidents full of tragedy and comedy to us, railroad and boat wrecks, late trains, fires that burned our hotels and opera houses, drives across the prairie in weather that registered forty below, being frozen in the straits of Northumberland—all accepted by Pauline Johnson as part of the game. She was, in truth a "Well Beloved Vagabond" who loved any trail, old or new.

CHAPTER IV

On the Road

As soon as Pauline began to achieve some success on the stage, her main ambition was to earn enough money to go to England, where she hoped to have a book of her poetry published. As early as 1894 this plan was realized.

London! Even in 1894 it was a city of more than six million people, the largest city in the world. Pauline delighted in its ancient stone buildings whose walls stored centuries of history. She looked in awe at its broad thoroughfares and listened to the sound of thousands of horsedrawn cabs clattering over the ancient cobblestones, alongside tramcars, and the newer electric railways. She visited Trafalgar Square and gazed at the stately government buildings, the monuments, and the beautiful fountains. She remained in London several months, continuing to give recitals. Finally, after seeing her book, *The White Wampum,* off to a successful start, she decided it was time to return home.

Pauline returned to Canada in the fall of 1894 and immediately arranged a tour that would take her into the United States and then all the way across Canada to the west coast. City after city, town after town, received and welcomed her. Her traveling was done mainly by train. On trains she read, or she wrote new poems and memorized them. Trains, hotels, and a stage performance nearly every evening made up her life.

As she traveled from place to place, she came to know the vast country that she felt was especially hers through her Indian ancestors, the first people to live on the land. From the Atlantic to the Pacific, Canada is an enormous country; each part of it has its special character. But Pauline, seeing it all from coast to coast, made it a part of herself. All of Canada was her homeland. Then, in turn, she gave Canadians a pride of country as she shared with her audiences the love she felt for her homeland.

Sometimes Pauline gave an evening's performance alone, but often she was part of a program that included others. In those days there were many performers on the concert circuit, dozens of whom had made reputations as fine artists in one way or another. Many of these performers became Pauline's friends.

One of these people who was to become a close friend as well as manager for Pauline's tours, was a man named Walter McRaye. He met Pauline in Winnipeg in 1897. Pauline, then thirty-five and near the peak of her career, was performing at the Winnipeg Theatre. Walter, just twenty at the time, described himself as a "stage-struck youth." He was also touring across Canada and the United States, giving recitations of William Henry Drummond's French-Canadian dialect poems. After the performance a friend took Walter backstage and introduced him to Pauline. Pauline suggested that they do some shows together, and they did so in Brandon, Portage la Prairie, and Morden. Pauline wanted to continue their association, but Walter had signed a contract for appearances in North Dakota and Montana that he could not cancel. So for the time being, they went their separate ways.

In 1899, Pauline met Walter McRaye again, and the two of them formed a partnership that lasted until Pauline's retirement from the stage. Walter took from Pauline's shoulders the burden of arranging the tours. He did all the bookings, made the financial arrangements, and took care of transportation. From this time on he became not only her manager, but also her constant companion and fellow performer.

One of their favorite areas of Canada was the Maritime Provinces, along the Atlantic coast. Nova Scotia was always a delight, but especially so in apple blossom time. In Anna-

Apple blossom time in Nova Scotia.

polis Valley there are acres and acres of apple orchards, and in the spring the fragrance of apple blossoms wafts over the countryside. The railroad on which Pauline and Walter traveled passed so close to the trees that she could almost reach out and pluck a blossom.

Part of Nova Scotia is known as Evangeline country, because it was the setting for Longfellow's famous poem, *Evangeline*. This land, once known as Acadia, was the earliest French colony in North America, settled sixteen years before the Pilgrims landed at Plymouth. The French planted apple trees and raised sheep and cattle on their neat, prosperous farms. Their influence still gives the area a special character, which Pauline loved and responded to. In later years she wrote an article called "The Orchards of Evangeline" in which she describes the "profound silence" of Acadia, whether the orchards were bursting with blossoms or heavy with fruit. For it seemed to her that Acadia always "dreams of past glories."

Pauline and Walter spent a summer on the island of Newfoundland, visiting all the fishing towns and the great cable station at a town named Heart's Content. They took a little old railway through villages with names like Blow-Me-Down, Witless Bay, Come-By-Chance, and Seldom-Come-By, where the smell of codfish drying on acres and acres of racks mingled with the fresh sea air. Here, too, they saw Newfoundland dogs with blocks of wood chained to their necks to prevent them from bothering the sheep. In visiting these small seaports, Pauline was not only giving recitals, but also gathering material for magazine articles she planned to write.

Pauline's name has sometimes been linked romantically

A portrait of Pauline taken in 1903, the same year her second book of poetry was published.

with that of Walter McRaye, but it is not known that they were anything else but coworkers and good companions. After Pauline retired, Walter married Lucy Webling, who was a close friend of both of them.

Pauline, Walter, and Lucy were good company for one another on the long train trips they took. To entertain themselves, they invented a set of imaginary little people they called "the boys." They began to talk to and about the boys as if they were real people. There were four of them, and they were supposed to have tiny mattresses with them which they put on the hatracks of the train. From their hideaway they could play all kinds of tricks and make impolite remarks. The boys always traveled with them and went to see all their performances.

Later, a group of imaginary animals was added. At one place in Nova Scotia the hotel had a cat that liked to sleep in Pauline's dressing bag. After that they pretended that the cat traveled with them, and they named it Dave Dougherty after the hotel owner. Then they added an imaginary bug named Felix Joggins and gave him a wife called Jerusha, who made Felix's life most trying. Still later, a mongoose known as Baraboo was added to the group. Baraboo, Felix and Jerusha Joggins, Dave Dougherty, and the boys had great fun and many exciting adventures together, not to mention keeping their three creators amused on their long trips across Canada.

As Pauline toured, she continued writing poetry, and she began to plan for a second book of verse. In 1903 her second book, *Canadian Born,* was published in Toronto. On the whole, the poems may be inferior as poetry to the poems in her first book, but *Canadian Born* was very popular, and the first edition sold out within the year. Pauline had intended the poems to touch the hearts of her fellow Canadians, and they expressed her growing love of Canada. In the book's preface, she wrote, "Let him who is Canadian born regard these poems as written to himself. . . . White race and Red are one if they are but Canadian born."

CHAPTER V

The West

Much as Pauline loved the Maritimes, she loved the West even more, and in a way seemed to be a part of it. In her day the Old West still had that freedom and romance which soon would come to an end. She and Walter gave entertainments in many towns that later became deserted. Other towns became modern cities.

Winnipeg, in the province of Manitoba, grew from a breezy frontier town to a metropolitan city in their lifetime. Winnipeg was built on the site of old Fort Garry. This fort, at the junction of the Red and the Assiniboine rivers, had been a supply point for the fur trade. The gate of the old fort still stands as a reminder of the place around which Winnipeg grew. In the 1890s Pauline and Walter still saw an occasional dog train, its sleds loaded with furs, going down the main street. Indians often sat on the steps of public buildings selling beadwork and buffalo horns, and cattlemen and their herds were never far away. The old Clarendon, Leland, and Manitoba hotels in Winnipeg came to be so familiar that they seemed like home to Pauline and Walter. All the employees knew and welcomed them.

Pauline and Walter crossed British Columbia, Alberta, Saskatchewan, and Manitoba again and again on their concert circuit. At length they were so well known that all they had to do by way of advance advertising was to send out a few postcards saying they were coming, and the local people did all the rest.

Regina, Saskatchewan, the "Queen City" of the plains, was named after Victoria Regina, Queen of England. It was also known as "Pile of Bones," because in presettlement days this was an Indian hunting ground where buffalo bones had accumulated.

East of Regina was Cannington Manor, a great estate owned by the Beckton brothers. Some unusual people for these parts, the Beckton brothers had come from England to the prairies in the early days. They were the sons of a wealthy English family and had plenty of money. They

Regina in Pauline Johnson's time. A typical visitor, wearing an Indian headdress and wrapped in a Hudson's Bay blanket, is crossing the street.

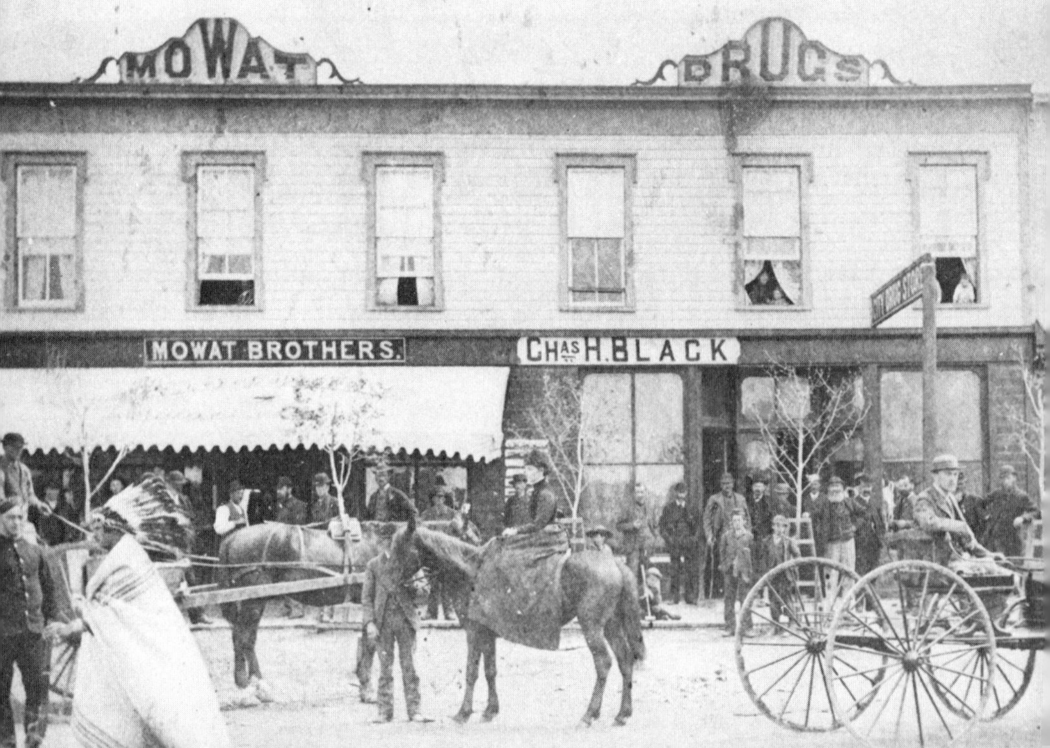

An elegant tennis party on the frontier. The Beckton brothers are making their guests feel at home.

built a large house that looked like an English castle, surrounded by tennis courts, cricket and polo grounds, and a race course. They even imported polo ponies and racing horses from England. With a number of servants to look after their needs, they gave many parties and entertained crowds of people.

The Becktons asked Pauline and Walter to come to their castle and entertain the guests there after a day of games. The two performers left the train at Moosomin, where they were met by a manservant who escorted them to a large horse-drawn carriage for the trip to the castle. Beside the driver sat two footmen wearing red coats. Walter wrote, "Thus we went across the prairie with outriders, and many were the cries of Tally Ho as we approached the home of the Becktons." The Becktons' guests liked their show so much that Pauline and Walter stayed two days.

In 1882 the Northwest Mounted Police had made Regina its headquarters. The force had been founded nine years earlier, in 1873, and its three hundred men checked frontier lawlessness and won the trust of the Indians. The Mounties did not welcome the outlaws and fortune hunters who were crossing the Canada/U.S. border into the vast hunting ground north of the Great Lakes that extended west to the Rockies. They sold whiskey to the thirty thousand Indians who still hunted the buffalo there and attacked them without reason. When Pauline and Walter made a trip into the United States, some friends they were visiting criticized the Mounties. Pauline defended them, pointing out their courage and trustworthiness. No doubt the fact that they had taken the side of the Indians in such situations was an important reason why Pauline felt so strongly. When she returned to Canada, she wrote a poem about the Mounties called "The Riders of the Plains." It praises the fearless fighters "Who never fail on the prairie trail 'neath the Territorial skies, / Who have laughed in the face of bullets and the edge of the rebels' steel, . . . / These are the famed that the North has named the 'Riders of the Plains' . . ."

Pauline's mind naturally ran to poetry, and often an incident she observed as they traveled along became the subject of a poem. One early spring morning in Edmonton, Pauline and Walter happened to see a train of sled dogs, driven by an Indian runner, coming down the street, headed for the fur trading store. The driver of the sled had been caught by the snow melt and now was traveling in the early morning on the frost, to finish the journey before the weather grew too warm. The scene is remembered in Pauline's poem, "The Train Dogs," which begins,

> Out of the night and the north,
>> Savage of breed and of bone,
> Shaggy and swift comes the yelping band
> Freighters of fur from the voiceless land
>> That sleeps in the Arctic zone.

Pauline and Walter always felt they were really getting west when they reached Calgary. Pinto ponies were usually tied to hitching posts along the street. Just ahead of the City of the Plains were the Rockies, swimming in the sunset— "Foothills to the Rockies lifting / Brown, and blue, and green, / Warm Alberta sunlight drifting / Over leagues between."

Many of Pauline's entertainments were given for charity. In one town the proceeds went to purchase a wooden leg for the town constable. Another time, in the very small town of Kuskanook, British Columbia, Pauline and Walter found that they had to spend the night waiting for train connections to take them through the Crow's Nest Pass down to Spokane, Washington. The town, according to Walter, "looked like a bundle of match boxes thrown carelessly against the hill." Among the town's two hundred people were six Methodists who wanted some kind of a building to use for a church. When they heard that Pauline was in town, they called on her and asked that she and Walter give a performance that evening for the cause.

Pauline said that she had never seen a place that looked more in need of a church, and she would be glad to help out.

A small boy was sent around the village ringing a bell and yelling, "Concert tonight. Concert tonight. Pauline Johnson. Pauline Johnson." Pauline found that her dressing "room" was a nook curtained off with Hudson's Bay blankets. The stage was a billiard table set across the corner of a room with a wooden soap box near it for a step. There on top of the billiard table Pauline and Walter gave a two-hour program for the benefit of the Methodist church.

In Nakusp, British Columbia, another act of kindness was almost a fatal mistake—fatal to a cow, that is. Tom Abriel, mayor of the town, owner of the local opera house, and president of "nearly everything," had asked them to perform. One lovely evening in June Pauline and Walter walked over early to the opera house. It was on the outskirts of town, next to a field of fresh green clover. Penned up on the other side of the fence was a lone cow looking hungrily at the clover. Pauline felt sorry for the animal. Not knowing that a cow's system cannot stand much of this rich fare at a time, she suggested to Walter that they open the gate and let the cow get into the clover. The next morning Mayor Abriel told Pauline that the cow had eaten herself sick and nearly died.

In August 1903, Pauline and Walter arrived in Vancouver, and they decided it was time to take a vacation. Their "vacation" was an eight-hundred mile trip up the Cariboo Trail, and they planned to give performances as they went! They had dreamed about this trip for a long time, and now the time seemed right.

The Cariboo Trail was famous as the way to the gold fields, which had been traveled during the 1860s by thousands of prospectors hoping to strike it rich. Most of them hadn't, and by the time Pauline traveled that road, it was a relic of past adventures. But the road was still good and the scenery spectacular. The trail was really a rocky shelf that ran for miles along the mountains, hundreds of feet above the Fraser River.

The Cariboo "Trail" looked more like a sturdy road by the time Pauline and Walter traveled on it.

A roadhouse on the trail where people rested while horses were changed.

The trail began at Ashcroft, where arrangements were made for a surrey drawn by a four-in-hand (four horses). The driver was Cariboo Billy, a tall, sun-tanned westerner, who wore a cowboy hat and a red kerchief around his neck.

That August was hot. Ashcroft was a sun-baked, dusty 104 degrees when they started out. Two thousand feet above them was the timberline. As they climbed, the air began to be cooler and more comfortable. Every twenty miles or so there was a roadhouse where they could get a meal and change horses. Pauline enjoyed hearing the names of each new team of horses as Cariboo Billy called them off: "Leaders, Buck and Brandy; wheelers, Luke and John."

Along the route Pauline and Walter gave performances

*At the end of the trail was Barkerville, which was almost
a ghost town when Pauline and Walter visited it.*

at several small towns. Barkerville was the high point of
this trip, not only because it was at the far end of the trail,
but also because the people there were so glad to have them
come. During the Gold Rush Barkerville had been built
quickly. The town was made up of miners' shacks, dance
halls, and one church. Now most of the shacks were empty,
the stores vacant, the wooden sidewalks rotting. There was
no traffic of any kind and stillness everywhere. Most of the
younger people had left, and the few older people who were
there lived quietly. Some of them had not been away from
the town to other parts of the province for forty years.

One of the next stops after Barkerville was a memorable
one for Pauline and Walter. After an eighty-mile drive with

the surrey and horses they wearily arrived at Lac la Hache late in the afternoon. News of their coming had been telegraphed ahead, and the people wanted an entertainment that same evening. Pauline and Walter did not see where an audience would come from in that place, but a rider on horseback went up and down the trail with the news, and soon the ranchers, miners, and Indians began to arrive. As always, people thought nothing of making a forty- or fifty-mile trip to attend a show when Pauline was the entertainer.

The performance was given in a large barnlike building on the edge of a silvery lake. A dance followed the show, attended by people who looked as if they might be in a western movie of today. There were ranchers in riding breeches, farmers in overalls, and a few women wearing their best dresses. Even the premier of British Columbia, Dick McBride, who happened to be in the area campaigning for re-election, was there. Walter was in full evening dress, and Pauline wore a silk brocade gown, which had a few oats still sticking to it as a result of her having to dress in an oat bin!

Pauline and Walter made a special side trip of about sixty miles to Lillooet, a beautiful townsite near the Fraser River. Rapids whirled down the canyon, and hundreds of feet above, they could see the wandering trail. Several years later, when Pauline was in England and longing for home, she remembered the trail to Lillooet and wrote a poem about the "Trail that winds and trail that wanders, like a cobweb hanging high, / Just a lazy thread outlining midway of the stream and sky." Such was the scenery of Pauline's beloved West.

CHAPTER VI

Three Chiefs

In 1906 Pauline decided to make a second trip to England. Canada had become much more important to England during the years since her first trip, and everyone Canadian was sure of a welcome. This time Walter went with her. They sailed on March 13, 1906.

Pauline had made many friends in London on her first visit, and after a twelve-year absence they greeted her warmly and invited her everywhere. The "drawing room entertainments," however, which had been so successful for Pauline, were no longer popular. Instead, she and Walter made their first London appearance at a large concert hall. Advertised as "E. Pauline Johnson—Tekahionwake, Indian Princess," she gave a performance that earned her very favorable reviews in the London newspapers.

While they were in London, Pauline and Walter had the opportunity to attend many fine plays. In the book he wrote later, Walter remarked, "Going to the theatre in London is different from New York and Canadian cities. There the theatre is not just a building or an auditorium, it is a fairy-land of make-believe. . . . The comfortable seats of the dress circle, the trim maids serving tea and sweets between the acts, the promenades, and the good manners of the audience, all make it something more than just being amused."

One of the plays they saw was *Land of Promise* by Somerset Maugham. It was set in Canada, But to Pauline and Walter it did not seem at all like Canada. Between acts Walter asked Pauline how she would like to be back on the trail in British Columbia. In answer, she turned over her theater program and wrote a poem on the back of it— "The Trail to Lillooet."

During the London season Pauline and Walter gave many recitals. Then in August they went on a holiday to a little town called Inkpen, Berkshire, where they rented rooms in an old house named Wellington Lodge. They found that most of the people in this small village had never been to London, eighty miles away. They had only the vaguest idea of what Canada was like, and they didn't quite believe what Pauline and Walter told them. "For example," Pauline said, "just one of Canada's many lakes, Lake Winnipeg, is 266 miles long, and if it were in England it would stretch from London to Newcastle, nearly the whole north-south length of England!" But the people of Inkpen were quite content with their thatched cottages, ivy-covered walls, and rose gardens.

While Pauline and Walter were in England, some other important visitors from Canada arrived in London—Chief Joe Capilano and two other Squamish chiefs from the Vancouver area. It seems that the Grand Trunk Pacific Railway had run its survey through the graves of their ancestors. The Squamish were worried that the railway might be built there, and they had also lost some of their ancient hunting and fishing rights. Since the Canadian government had not made an effort to help them, the Indians of Vancouver had

The thatched cottages that Pauline and Walter admired can still be seen in Inkpen today.

held a potlatch, a great feast at which many kinds of food were served and gifts were handed out. At the potlatch, the decision had been made that three of their chiefs should go to England to talk with the king. Officials of the British government did not know what to do about them and were waiting for instructions from Ottawa, the Canadian capital. The chiefs were lonely and puzzled because they were not being taken to the king. They knew one thing: they had come five thousand miles to see him, and they were going to do it.

About this time Pauline was writing some articles about Indians for one of the London newspapers. The editor heard about the three chiefs from Vancouver, and he suggested that Pauline talk to them. A meeting was arranged, and a reporter was present to write up the event as a feature article.

"Klahoya tillicum scookum!" exclaimed Pauline as she walked to Joe Capilano with her hand outstretched. Pauline had learned this West Coast Indian greeting during her visits to Vancouver. The chiefs were delighted to hear these familiar words so far from British Columbia. Large headlines appeared on the front page of the next day's newspaper, describing the meeting. Perhaps the king and queen read it, for not long afterwards, the three chiefs were received by King Edward VII and Queen Alexandra at Buckingham Palace.

The king and queen showed great kindness in dealing with these Canadian subjects. The Indians had brought a gift of woven baskets for the queen. When a lady-in-waiting stepped forward to take them, the queen said that she would receive them herself. She told Chief Joe that she

The "mighty arches" of St. Paul's Cathedral in London.

would use the baskets when she took her grandchildren on picnics. Chief Joe was very impressed with his visit to Buckingham Palace. He told Pauline, "In this world there are two kinds of men. The first kind stands still when you meet him and makes you come to him. The second kind steps forward and shakes your hand. The king is the second kind."

Pauline saw Chief Joe several more times in London, and three years later she renewed her friendship with him in Vancouver. It was from Joe Capilano that Pauline learned many of the Indian legends that she later put into her book, *Legends of Vancouver*.

Among the articles Pauline wrote for one of the London papers was "A Pagan in St. Paul's," in which she expresses the thoughts of an Indian visiting this great cathedral. She wrote that as she listened to the music, "it swept up those mighty arches until the grey dome above me faded, and in its place the stars came out to look down, not on these . . . kneeling worshipers, but on . . . my own people in my own land, who also assembled to do honour to the Manitou of all nations. . . . The altar lights of St. Paul's glowed for me no more. In their place flared the camp fires of the Onondagas' 'long house.' . . . . I lift my head which had been bowed on the chair before me. It is St. Paul's after all, and the clear boy-voices rise above the rich echoes of the organ."

CHAPTER VII

Vancouver

The years of constant travel were beginning to tell on Pauline's health. By 1909 she was forty-eight, and she was longing for some rest and quiet time to read and write. Where was her resting place to be? Every city, town, and village of her native land knew and loved her. She felt they were all familiar, but the place she loved best was Vancouver. She had been there about a dozen different times in her travels, and now she chose to go there for good. Walter made the arrangements for her travel across the Rockies, and they gave a "good-bye performance" in Kamloops, British Columbia. Then she and Walter parted. Pauline put away her battered old steamer trunk and settled down in an apartment in Vancouver. Walter continued on the entertainment circuit with Lucy Webling, whom he soon married.

One of the things Pauline was eager to do after she ended her touring was to collect all her poems in one volume. This complete edition of her poems was, in a sense, her gift to the Canadian people. Published in 1912, it was entitled *Flint and Feather.* Her two previous books of poetry, *The White Wampum* and *Canadian Born,* made up the first two sections of *Flint and Feather.* The third section is made up of other poems that were either not used in the first two books or written later.

Besides poetry, Pauline also wrote a number of stories. Some were stories about Indian children written for a magazine called *Boys' World*. These stories served as preparation for more important work to come. The first year that she lived in Vancouver, Chief Joe Capilano told her many stories of his tribe, the Squamish. Most of them were tales that had been handed down by word of mouth from ancient times. Pauline added some stories of the Iroquois and wrote down these legends with the skill of a master storyteller. Originally, these delightful stories were printed in magazines, but later, they were collected into the book *Legends of Vancouver*. Today, she is as well known for this book as for her poetry.

One of Pauline's favorite legends is the story of Siwash Rock, which still stands on the edge of Stanley Park in Vancouver, looking out to the sea. One day when she and Chief Joe were paddling their canoe by the rock, he asked if she knew how it came to be there. She did not, and he told her the story, which she later retold for her readers.

A young chief and his wife were expecting a child. On the day that it was to be born, the parents went down to the Narrows to swim in the sea. It was the custom that the parents of a coming child must swim until they were so clean that wild animals could not pick up their scent. If the creatures of the forest had no fear of them, then, and only then, were they fit to become parents. The woman slipped away into the forest, and while the baby was being born, the man stayed in the sea. "If he did not swim hour after hour," Pauline wrote, "his child would come to an unclean father. He must give his child a chance in life; he must not hamper it by his own uncleanliness at its birth."

As he swam, a great canoe bearing four men came up the Narrows. They were sent from the Sagalie Tyee (the Great Spirit), they told him, and they ordered him to leave the water. The young man refused.

"I dare anything for the cleanliness and purity of my coming child," he said. "My child must be born to a spotless life."

While those sent from the Great Spirit talked among themselves about what they should do, a baby's cry rose from the forest. The leader of the men stood up and faced the rising sun. He chanted a promise.

"You have placed that child's future before all things, and for this the Sagalie Tyee commands us to make you forever a pattern for your tribe. You shall never die, but you shall stand through all the thousands of years to come, where all eyes can see you."

The moment the young man stepped ashore, he was changed into a great rock. His wife and child were also transformed so they could be near him. A large rock with a small rock beside it stands close to Siwash Rock.

Chief Joe died about a year after Pauline's retirement to Vancouver, and she felt the loss of this good friend very keenly.

As she worked, Pauline was becoming more and more ill. She kept writing, although at times she was in pain. She did not consult a doctor until some time after her arrival in Vancouver, and then only at the urging of a friend. It was discovered that she had cancer, which was by that time far advanced.

Pauline (left) visits with Walter's wife, Lucy, in this last photo taken of her.

Pauline felt she was writing against time. Not only did she want to finish her work for its own sake, but she badly needed the money. She had never earned a great deal more than her living expenses, and when she did have a little extra, she had shared it with someone else. The legends, when they were sold one by one to magazines, brought in only a few dollars each, not nearly enough for her to live on.

Pauline tried giving a few last recitals in Vancouver, but she did not have the strength. A few days before the last one was scheduled, she sent word she could not make it. Two young women, who knew about Pauline's problems, decided that the concert would be given by someone else, so the proceeds could go to Pauline. They found some local talent to put on the performance and sold enough tickets to fill the house. The day after the show they brought a box of strawberries to Pauline, telling her that the best berries were underneath. When she looked for them, she found on the bottom of the box a layer of gold pieces, which they explained was the money from the concert she had missed. Tears filled her eyes in gratitude for such kindness.

Now Pauline's friends got together to plan how her writing could be used to provide money for her. Beginning with a small group of newspaper people, this "committee" of friends grew until it included many people in Vancouver, and indeed, throughout Canada. They wanted to collect and publish Pauline's Indian legends in book form. She was so proud that only from a business deal such as this would she accept financial help.

The group began by raising funds until they had enough for a first printing of a thousand copies of *Legends of Van-*

couver. At this time Walter McRaye returned to Vancouver, and he acted as sales manager for the book. As a result of his campaign, enough money was raised to finance a second printing of ten thousand copies. All of the income above the cost of printing was paid into Pauline's account. Soon orders were coming in steadily. The many cheerful letters that came in with the orders helped Pauline through a difficult time. And now there was enough money to support her comfortably.

Finally, Pauline had to go to the hospital. Walter made plans for her to enter the Bute Street Hospital, a private nursing home. She had a little room on the second floor where she could have some of her own things around her, and she was free to come and go as she pleased.

Visits from friends made her very happy. One of the old friends who visited Pauline was Arthur, Duke of Connaught, who was now governor-general of Canada. Arrangements were made ahead for his coming. The hospital was decorated with plants and flowers, and Pauline wore a new blue and gold robe, a gift from friends for this special occasion. Pauline remembered the old scarlet blanket on which the duke had stood when he was made a chief of the Six Nations, and which she had worn as part of her costume. Now she draped it over the chair on which he would sit. The matron ushered the distinguished guest upstairs, and he and Pauline visited alone for half an hour. As her parting gift to him, Pauline had ready a copy of *Flint and Feathers* especially bound in blue suede with a silver decoration on the cover. She had dedicated this collection of poems to him, in honor of his position as "Head Chief of the Six Nations Indians."

In October Walter thought she ought to have a member

of her family with her, and he sent for her sister Evelyn. Evelyn came with the idea of taking Pauline back to Brantford. She felt that Pauline should spend her last days in her old home. But Pauline refused to consider such a move. She did not want to be "dragged back," as she put it, to Brantford. She wanted to stay in Vancouver, and said she would die happy if she could be buried in Stanley Park, near the sound of the sea breaking against Siwash Rock.

Pauline never spoke of fear or regret for the life she would be leaving. She told her friends she did not want them to mourn for her. "If now and again the people of Canada read some line of my work which brings home to them my love for this great country," she said, "I hope they remember me as having done my best to share something which the Great Spirit gave to me."

Pauline died on March 7, 1913, at the age of fifty-two. Walter was with her at the end. Her funeral was almost an affair of state, which was attended by many Canadian leaders, including the Squamish Indian chiefs. Flags flew at half-mast throughout the city. With the help of the Duke of Connaught, special permission was granted for the urn containing Pauline's ashes to be buried in Stanley Park near Siwash Rock and the sea. A simple stone monument was placed there, engraved simply with her name, Pauline. Since 1922, a second monument has stood in Stanley Park, next to the original stone. A profile of Pauline's face is carved on this monument, along with the prow of a canoe, a feather, and a flint-tipped arrow.

Since Pauline's death, various literary critics have tried to decide whether or not she was a really great poet. Some say that while she was without doubt Canada's best Indian

The funeral procession for Pauline Johnson in Vancouver.

poet, her work does not measure up to that of many other great poets. Some feel that her success lay more in her dramatic ability and her personality, than in the quality of her poems. Others credit her work as unusual in that it blends Indian tradition with Western style. She expresses the deepest feelings of the Indian in Indian rhythm and Indian imagery, yet her lyric poetry is in the style of the English poets whom she studied and loved from her childhood days at Chiefswood. Critics generally agree that the reason her poems were put into Canadian school textbooks and anthologies during the 1920s was that, at the time, there was a growing interest in literature written by Canadians.

Pauline herself was not concerned about whether her poems were "great." She wanted to speak for the Indian people, and she wanted to express her love for her country, Canada. These things she did. Her desire was to be remembered as an Indian, whose life and writings were devoted to her people. "Forget that I was Pauline Johnson," she wrote, "but remember that I was Tekahionwake, the Mohawk that humbly aspired to be the saga singer of her people."

There was a period when interest in Pauline's poetry nearly died out, but in 1961, the hundredth anniversary of her birth, there was a revival of interest in Pauline Johnson. The government issued a Pauline Johnson stamp that was available at all post offices in Canada. It was the first stamp recognizing a Canadian Indian, and the first in honor of any woman who was not a member of the royal family. In Vancouver, a memorial service was held at her grave in Stanley Park, signaled by the firing of the famous "nine o'clock gun." This gun is an antique muzzle loader mounted

Two members of the Squamish tribe, one a descendant of Pauline's friend, Chief Joe Capilano, honor her memory at services held by her grave in 1961.

near Brockton Point in Stanley Park. It is the custom to fire it at nine o'clock every evening. This time, tradition was broken when the gun was fired at two o'clock to open the service. "The Song My Paddle Sings" was recited to the audience that had gathered to remember and honor her.

In Brantford, Pauline's birthday was observed by a simple ceremony held at Chiefswood. At that time the house was in the process of being restored by the Six Nations Council as a historic site. The restoration was completed in 1963, and today the house is open to tour groups.

Pauline Johnson, for what she did and for what she was, had her place as a poet and as an entertainer in the hearts of her fellow Canadians, both Indian and white. She traveled as few others have done, to nearly every town in Canada, writing poetry as she went and speaking out on behalf of the Indian people. Through the sheer force of her personality, she became well known and well loved throughout the length and breadth of a great country. For that she is still remembered and honored.

The photographs are reproduced through the courtesy of
the Brant County Museum; the British Columbia
Provincial Archives; the British Tourist Authority; the
City Archives, Vancouver, British Columbia; the New
York State Museum and Science Service; the Nova
Scotia Communications and Information Center; the
Public Archives of Canada; the Saskatchewan Archives;
and the Vancouver Public Library.

Quotations from *Pauline Johnson and her Friends* by
Walter McRaye are used with permission of the publisher,
McGraw-Hill Ryerson, Ltd., Scarborough, Ontario.
"The Siwash Rock," a tale in *Legends of Vancouver* by
Pauline Johnson, has been retold by permission of the
Canadian publisher, McClelland and Stewart, Ltd.,
Toronto, Canada.

THE AUTHOR

Lucie K. Hartley, a freelance writer and journalist, has long had an interest in history. She is the author of *The Carver Story,* a history of Carver, Minnesota. While doing research for this book, she visited the area in Ontario where Pauline Johnson grew up.

A *cum laude* graduate of the University of Minnesota, Mrs. Hartley has been an elementary school teacher and principal. She has also written *Maria Sanford, Pioneer Professor* for Dillon Press.